THINK THEOLOGICALLY about Money

Sarah Arthur

Cover Design: Keely Moore

MANUFACTURED IN THE UNITED STATES OF AMERICA

04 05 06 07 08 09 10 11 12 13—10 9 8 7 6 5 4 3 2 1

CONTENTS

Writer Bio

A former youth director, Sarah F. Arthur now serves youth as an author, editor, speaker, and workshop leader. In addition to writing *Thinking Theologically About Money* and *Thinking Theologically About Pop Culture,* Sarah has written curriculum for *LinC* and *Claim the Name.* Her first book, *Walking With Frodo: A Devotional Journey Through the Lord of the Rings,* is one of the first in Tyndale House Publisher's new Thirsty line for young adults. She also writes fiction and poetry and illustrates her own stories for children. Check out her work on *www.saraharthur.com.* Sarah and her husband, Tom, live in Petoskey, Michigan.

Why Teach Thinking Theologically?

So what is **"thinking theologically"**? It means being able to look at things from God's perspective and acting accordingly (*theo* = "god"; *ology* = "the study of"). The theological framework we will use comes from an eighteenth century Anglican minister named John Wesley. He encouraged his congregations to assess any topic, using four anchor points: Scripture, experience, reason, and tradition. One of these four points will be tackled each session, with a "jump-start" session to introduce the topic and a "wrap-up" session to bring closure.

Why? Because our teens are drifting, with no clear idea as to their real destination: salvation and holiness through Jesus Christ. You, as their teacher, are in many ways like the captain of a ship, charting a course for your students that will allow them to navigate from harbor to harbor in safety. Unfortunately, the values of our culture are like a fog shrouding the spiritual coastline: the longer our teens stay in it, the less sure they are about their location and destination. Use the "Prayer Notes" in the margins each week, and pray for the Holy Spirit to blow the fog away.

How? By teaching the students a method for "thinking theologically" about any topic and by involving them in weekly worship rituals that remind them of their faith heritage. Each session is self-contained but is also carefully linked to all the other sessions through the weekly review of the major theological points.

Thinking theologically about money is a **different approach** to a topical study for senior highs. But this way of talking about life issues grounds youth squarely in faith. A primary lesson from the study will be a way to make faithful decisions now and throughout life.

Every session includes **multiple options** that allow you to cater to the different learning styles in your group. For the debate team champion, there are intellectual challenges. For the basketball player and the kid who is barely awake, the more active and creative options might do the trick. You be the judge.

The opening and closing **worship rituals** are the same for every session throughout the entire series. Students hear the Word, learn it, and retain it, providing a reservoir of Living Water from which to draw in dry times.

The **student book** is designed for both information and transformation. It gives the major points of each session, and then it helps youth process what they have learned in a way that leads to spiritual growth. For this reason, the students should put their name on the inside cover of their book so that they can use the same book from week to week. When the study is finished, the students can take the book home as a reminder of all they learned and experienced.

Spend **six weeks**, or spread the sessions out over as many weeks as you want.

For the most part, the study requires only the **typical supplies** of a Sunday school classroom, plus a student book for each youth.

You will need a student book for each participant. Keep these in the classroom from week to week until the study is done. You might also want to have several extra student books on hand just in case.

1

THINKING THEOLOGICALLY

Goals for this Session

To introduce students to the importance of thinking theologically about issues.

To give them a tool to use and practice to help them think theologically about issues, specifically money.

"Prayer does not fit us for the greater work; prayer is the greater work."

—Oswald Chambers, in *My Utmost for His Highest*

Activity	Time	Preparation	Supplies
GATHERING			
True Confessions	7–10 minutes	Gather supplies.	dice, posterboard or butcher paper, markers
Sticky-Note Ritual	3–5 minutes	None	student books
Thinking Theologically	7–10 minutes	None	student books
DIVING IN			
Internet Challenge	15–25 minutes	None	student books, Bibles, paper, pencils
Brand-Name Challenge	15–25 minutes	Visit the websites listed in the margin on page 3 to gain some background on the use of sweatshop labor. If you know students who have Internet access, ask them to do some of the research.	computer with Internet access, student books
CLOSING			
Think About It	7–15 minutes	None	student books
Worship	3–5 minutes	None	student books

Prayer Notes

Prayers for the students and their families . . .

Prayers for myself . . .

Prayers for the message itself to have an impact . . .

Other concerns . . .

True Confessions

As students arrive, invite them into a "true confessions" conversation. Ask the group some or all of these questions; keep the tone light. Have the students take turns throwing a die to choose one of the six questions, if you prefer.

1. What is your first memory of money?
2. What is your favorite store?
3. What is the worst thing you ever spent money on?
4. What is the best thing you ever spent money on?
5. What's on your Christmas list?
6. If you were given one million dollars, how would you spend it?

OPTIONAL GROUP COVENANT: Using a die, have each student make a toss then answer the question below that corresponds to the number rolled.

1. I get annoyed when the teacher . . .
2. It annoys me in class when a student . . .
3. My most embarrassing classroom memory is . . .
4. My favorite memory of Sunday school is . . .
5. Sunday school would be really interesting if . . .
6. The perfect Sunday school experience would be . . .

After several rounds, say: "Well, we've gotten to know one another a little bit. We have discovered not only our various ideas about money, but also what we think makes for a good classroom experience. So let's take the information and create a covenant, or set of promises, that states how we will act together so that we can have the best possible class experience. What needs to be on this covenant?"

Using posterboard or butcher paper, write out (or have a student write out) what the class comes up with. Then have everyone sign the covenant.

Sticky-Note Ritual

Invite the class to turn to page 6 in the student book. Have a student read aloud "Sticky-Note Rituals."

Then say, "Each time, when we begin class, someone will read the leader's part, and the class will respond. Toward the end of this study, we should know this ritual by heart."

Have the class try this several times, using different leaders. Then have them join you in prayer, which can be student-led or ad-libbed, or use this one:

Dear Lord, as we start a new class on the topic of money, help us to know that everything we have comes from you. Nothing we have belongs to us, but is yours to use as you please. We are merely stewards of your treasures. Help us to set aside our greed and our pride and instead to offer ourselves and our wealth to you in humility and trust. In the name of Jesus Christ, Amen.

If your group members are new to one another, follow the initial activity with creating a class covenant.

Thinking Theologically About . . .

Thinking Theologically

Introduce the approach to this study, using the material on pages 7–10 in the student book. You have several options:

A. Have students take turns reading the material aloud.
B. Have the students skim it while you summarize key points.
C. Use questions to find out what students already know and then elaborate upon their knowledge.
D. Use a combination of A, B, and C.

Diving In

The two challenges in the student book (Internet Challenge, pages 11–13, and Brand Name Challenge, pages 14–15) provide opportunities for the students to try thinking theologically about money, using the Quadrilateral approach. The four-fold theological framework is meant to be practical and useful. The challenges will also help students understand that even the simplest of topics may have no easy answers, even from a Christian perspective.

Use one or both of the challenges as your time and interest dictate. You may choose to spend more than one class period if you would like to do both.

Internet Challenge

Read the challenge, page 11 in the student book. Have the students look up the Scripture references given (John 14:15, 21; and 15:10). What do they say?

Divide the students into four groups; assign each team one of the four sections of the Quadrilateral and the questions in the student book.

After a few minutes, come back together. Have each group report and give their recommendation. Invite the others to add to the discussion. At the conclusion of each section, ask for vote of the group. How many would give the guy $10? Keep a record of the numbers.

Discuss the "Finally" questions and the quotation from Mother Teresa, on page 13 of the student book.

Brand-Name Challenge

Before class: You may find it helpful to visit the websites listed in the margin to gain some background on this issue of the use of sweatshop labor. If you know students who have Internet access, think about contacting them during the week to ask them to do some of the research.

Read John 14:15, 21; and 15:10.

www.sweatshopwatch.org
www.nikewages.org.

Read the challenge and fill in or have your student researchers fill in some of the background. For example, do your youth know what a sweatshop is?

Divide the students into four groups; assign each team one of the four sections of the Quadrilateral and the questions in the student book. If you have a large class, consider assigning multiple teams of no more than four to the same section of the Quadrilateral.

After a few minutes, come back together. Have each group report and give their recommendation. Invite the others to add to the discussion. At the conclusion of each section ask for vote of the group. Should they or should they not buy brand name items made in sweatshop conditions? Keep a record of the numbers.

Discuss the "Finally" question on page 15 of the student book. Also ask these questions or roleplay such situations:

- If you choose not to wear brand name items, how will you defend your decision to your non-Christian friends—from a Christian perspective?
- If you choose to wear brand name items, how will you defend your decision to your Christian friends—from a Christian perspective?

Encourage your students to think twice the next time they go shopping.

Closing

Think About It

Have students look over the "Think About It" points on page 16. Ask various students which one of the statements they feel most strongly about and why. Encourage them to make a connection to the discussions around the challenge they faced or with their own beliefs and money-use choices.

Worship

You may want to invite a student to lead the closing worship next week.

Let the group know that you are excited about what will be happening in next few weeks (don't hesitate to tell the plan for the class), and that you are looking forward to what God will be doing in each of their lives as you go through this study together.

Ask whether students have any prayer requests before you pray together. You may invite a student to lead the prayer or do it yourself.

If your class has a closing ritual, you may decide to continue using it. If not, try this one:

Close with the class saying together the same benediction every week (found on page 6 in the student book):

Together: May "the grace of the Lord Jesus Christ, the love of God, and the fellowship of the Holy Spirit be with all of you." Amen.

—2 Corinthians 13:14

If you have time, work together on memorizing the benediction before the students leave.

THINKING THEOLOGICALLY

Experience

Goals for this Session

To offer students hands-on or testimonial experience about the negative and positive effects of money.

To examine attitudes toward persons based on their financial resources.

Prayer frees us to be controlled by God. To pray is to change. There is no greater liberating force in the Christian life than prayer.

—Richard Foster, in *Freedom of Simplicity*

Prayer Notes

Prayers for the students and their families . . .

Activity	Time	Preparation	Supplies
GATHERING			
What's Cool?	8–15 minutes	Prepare a timeline on large sheets of paper (see page 6).	large sheets of paper, markers or crayons, tape
Sticky-Note Ritual	3–4 minutes	None	student books
Thinking Theologically	7–10 minutes	None	student books
DIVING IN			
OPTION 1 **The American Game**	20–30 minutes	Prepare the game pieces, on pages 11–14, as directed.	student books
OPTION 2 **Panel Discussion or Guest Speaker**	15–25 minutes	Arrange to have a guest or guests who will discuss personal experiences with debt. This should be done several weeks in advance of this session.	none
CLOSING			
Think About It	7–15 minutes	None	student books
Worship	3–5 minutes	None	student books

Prayers for myself . . .

Prayers for the message itself to have an impact . . .

Other concerns . . .

What's Cool?

Before students arrive, create a timeline on large sheets of paper. Title the timeline "What I Wanted for Christmas," then put the following headings horizontally from left to right along the time continuum: "first grade," "third grade," "fifth grade," "seventh grade," and so on. Tape or tack the timeline on the wall and have crayons or markers on hand. As students arrive, invite them to fill in the timeline to the best of their memory. Afterward discuss:

• Did you get what you wanted for Christmas when you were in [first grade]? Why, or why not?

• How long did your Christmas gifts satisfy you before you wanted something else?

• What does that tell you about the human desire for things?

Sticky-Note Ritual

Refer the students to page 6 in the student book and their sticky-notes. Together recite the opening psalm.

Leader: "O give thanks to the LORD, for [God] is good,"

Class: "for [God's] steadfast love endures forever." (Psalm 136:1)

Join briefly in prayer. This can be student-led or ad-libbed, or you can use the following:

Dear Lord, as we experience various ways that money has an impact on our lives for evil as well as for good, show us how we are to be wise stewards of all you have given us. Give us courage to be obedient to you in our use of money, that we may be spared the kind of heartache that comes from foolish debt, and so that our money can be used in ways that glorify you and advance your kingdom. (If applicable): Bless our guest(s) as they share their story with us, and help us to support and encourage them in their journey with you. For the sake of your Son, our Savior, Jesus Christ, Amen.

Thinking Theologically

It is not likely that everyone in class today was there last week, so it is important to briefly review all that you learned.

If your class created a covenant (page 2), spend some time going over it. Invite the new students to sign it (2–3 minutes).

Turn to page 9 of the student book for review of the four sections of the "Wesleyan Quadrilateral." You may want to draw a box and label the four quadrants to help students have visual reminder of the Quadrilateral. Spend some time with "Things to Keep in Mind" (page 10).

Ask, "Why should we use all four components of the Quadrilateral when discerning the truth—not just reason or experience alone?"

Thinking Theologically About ...

Explore the limits of each section. Be sure to point out that John Wesley felt that Scripture was more authoritative than the other three.

To summarize, you might say: "We must put all four components of the Quadrilateral together to get a comprehensive Christian understanding of any topic, including money. So today we are going to look at 'experience.' What has been the human experience with money? What has been your experience with money? How can we learn from these experiences?"

Diving In

In this section you have two options: The American Game or a panel or guest speaker. Choose based on your interest, time, and available resources. Also, feel free to use more than one option if you would like to expand this study.

OPTION 1 → The American Game

The following game is designed to show the great disparities between the poor, the middle class, and the rich in the United States. It will also help youth experience how difficult it is for those who are born in poverty to rise out of their circumstances.

The game should be done in classes of six or more, with at least one other adult or older student assisting. Split the class into three equal groups, keeping in mind group dynamics.

One group represents the lower class (A), one the middle class (B), and one the upper class (C). Do not tell the students these distinctions. Using any symbol, number, or letter you wish to designate groups, write their group designation in marker on their left or right hand, or give them a card or bracelet showing to which group they belong.

Establish your "Bank." This is your adult or student helper who will distribute money to the students on "Pay Day" and sell them the items of their choice during other rounds. Depending on the size of your class, you may want to have three "Banks," one for each group. Each "Bank" needs a copy of Bankers' Rules (Reproducible Resource 1, page 11), explaining which groups receive which amounts of money at each round, and how much different items are worth.

Each "Bank" needs to be well equipped with play money (available in other games or from most dollar stores; or easily created by writing out denominations on plain paper, running it through a copier, and cutting it to size).

The "Banks" also have "Proof of Purchase" cards representing each item for sale (see Reproducible Resource 3, page 13) as well as "That's Life" cards (see Reproducible Resource 4, page 14) stacked face-down in a pile. Students draw these during Round 7.

Give the students each the Cost of Living lists or just make one for each group (see Reproducible Resource 3, page 13).

Feel free to add a new "That's Life" scenario of your own making.

Before you play the game, give the following instructions: "Welcome to the American Game. The object of this game is for you to be as successful as you can in life using the money you are given, to gain as much stuff as you can. We will play this game in a series of rounds in which you go to the Bank (point to the Bank and your trusty bankers) for your paycheck and then have a chance to shop for the things you need and want. Please remember: you must pay for food and rent every time, no exceptions. The only way you get to stop paying rent is if you buy a house. Also, you may improve your situation in lots of creative ways, but stealing from others or from the Bank gets you automatically disqualified! During one round, everyone must select a 'That's Life' card, which represents a real-life circumstance outside of your control. You must do whatever the 'That's Life' card says. So let's open the game with the first round. Everyone needs to go to the Bank to receive your starting amounts of money."

Let the game begin. Follow the order of rounds according to Rounds of Play (Reproducible Resource 2, page 12).

Town Meeting (Optional) Ask if anyone has any questions. For example, Group C may want to know whether they may buy more than one car, education, or house, for example. (The answer is yes.) Group A on the other hand, may want to know how it is that the other groups get so much more money ("That's just how the game is played").

You may also ask the question, What would happen if people started pooling their resources? Some students may ask about getting married or being roommates. (Charge couples $20 to marry, and inform them that a divorce costs $30. They may combine their food, rent, and car costs. If someone marries another person who already owns a house, he or she no longer has to pay rent. There is no charge for becoming roommates; however, they may only split the cost of housing but not food or transportation.) Students may also decide to carpool, give money directly to someone who needs it, create a commune, or do whatever else they think of.

For the final round of Town Meeting, ask:
- What was going on with the three different groups? How is that like life? (You may want to point out that if the game were to really be like life around the world, only 16% of the students would be in the "upper class," 28% in the "middle class," and 56% in the "lower class" [From *The State of the World Atlas*, by Dan Smith].)

- What was it like to be in the lowest group, earning the least? What frustrated you the most about it? What, if anything, did anyone do for you that helped your circumstances? What could people have done to help you out? How were you affected by your "That's Life" card?

- What was it like in the middle group, earning a middle income? How were you affected by your "That's Life" card?

- What was it like to be in the highest group, earning the most? What did you like best about it? What was your response when you learned other people were earning less? How difficult do you think it would be to help one of the people with less get a car? Buy a house? Get a college education? How were you affected by your "That's Life" card?

Use either the "town meeting" format or simply answer such questions as they occur and dispense information as needed, especially if the frustration level rises in the group.

Be sure to leave time for the final round Town Meeting. It is an opportunity to process the experience and learn from it.

Thinking Theologically About ...

These are highly likely to be results of the game:

• No matter how hard the lower class worked, they could barely stay afloat. Getting a college education or a house was clearly out of the question. Some of them were extremely frustrated and even felt angry as the game progressed and they watched what the other groups could do. Some even contemplated breaking the law! But when offered help, they had mixed emotions of embarrassment, relief, and bitterness.

• The middle class hung on fairly well, but they still had to sacrifice to buy the more costly things. They often spent several rounds saving up before they could. They were glad to not be in the lower class but probably felt very nervous about giving any money away because it would keep them from accomplishing some of their own plans. They likely felt jealous of the upper class, and wished they could have all that stuff too. Depending on their "That's Life" card, they could very easily plunge into the lower group's situation and would struggle to make their way up again.

• The upper class had the best head start on everybody, and in just a few rounds they were able to spend money on extra things and entertainment, just because they could. Several of them found the circumstances of the others something to laugh at, while others just didn't care. Some wanted to help. Their "That's Life" cards really didn't affect them all that much. What does Jesus have to say to those who are rich? (Mark 10:21-27)

If these points don't come out in the discussion, you may want to pursue them further with the youth.

To summarize, turn to page 17 in the student book, and spend some time answering the questions for reflection.

OPTION 2 Panel Discussion or Guest Speaker

This option requires preparation several weeks in advance as you invite a person or persons within your church to speak about personal experiences with debt. The guests need to be mature adults who are open to discussing this issue publicly and are comfortable talking with a classroom of teenagers. These people should also have the ability to speak about this issue in the context of their Christian faith.

You may wish to use an interview style, in which you ask a question (or the students ask a question) and the guest responds. Or you may have each guest prepare a 5– to 7–minute testimony, with the chance for the class to ask questions afterward. It may be helpful to have each guest leave when he or she is finished so that your class has time to process what was discussed without feeling inhibited.

Begin by introducing each guest and explaining why the guests are in class today. (Make sure that you do not set up guests to be uncomfortable, and make sure that your facts are straight.) Then give your guest(s) the floor. Some panel or interview questions might be:

• How did you get into debt?

• When did you realize things needed to change?

• What did you do (or are you doing) to get out of debt?

- How long did (or will) it take?

- What will you do now to stay out of debt?

- How does your Christian faith help you make financial decisions?

- If you could tell young people one thing about debt, what would it be?

Once the guest(s) have left, reflect together. What did the guest say that was most startling or that will have the greatest impact on the students' views of money? What did the students learn that they might not have known before? After hearing the testimonies, what do the students think now about going into debt?

Think About It!

Using page 18 of the student book, take some time to review what you discussed in class, including the reasons for using all four parts of the Quadrilateral (student book pages 9 and 10).

Worship

Let your students know that you are excited about what will be happening next week (don't hesitate to tell about the plan for the series) and that you are looking forward to what God will be doing in each of their lives as you go through this study together. Ask whether any of the class members have prayer requests before inviting a student to lead the prayer.

Close with the liturgy from the student book, page 6.

Together: May "the grace of the Lord Jesus Christ, the love of God, and the fellowship of the Holy Spirit be with all of you." Amen.
—2 Corinthians 13:14

Bankers' Rules

Starting Pay

Bankers hand out starting amounts one at a time to individual members of each group. All students must prove which group they belong to before receiving money.

> Group A—$30
> Group B—$60
> Group C—$100

Shopping

Students are allowed to purchase any of the below items as long as they have the money. They may not borrow from the Bank. Once they tell the banker what they wish to purchase, the banker collects the money and hands them the appropriate card.

> Entertainment—$5
>
> Food—$10 (not optional)
>
> Rent—$20 (not optional unless you have a house). If you don't pay your rent for three rounds (consecutive or not), you are evicted.
>
> Car—$30 (Once the student owns a car, he or she receives $5 extra on Payday)
>
> College Education—$80 (Once the student has a college education, she or he receives $20 extra on Payday)
>
> House—$90 (Once the student owns a house, he or she does not have to pay rent; but he or she must pay the mortgage.)
>
> Retirement—$100 (must have house first)

Payday

Students come to the Bank to receive their pay. They must prove which group they are in before they receive payment. They must also show any cards representing items that have earned them extra pay ($5 for each car, $20 for each college education).

Group	Basic Pay	W/ Car	W/ College	W/ Car & College
A	$20	$25	$40	$45
B	$50	$55	$70	$75
C	$80	$85	$100	$105

Rounds of Play

Give at least one copy of this page to each group.

Round 1: Starting Pay

Round 2: Shopping
Visit the Bank to make your purchases.

Round 3: Payday
Visit the Bank to receive your pay.

Round 4: Shopping

Town Meeting (optional)

The optional Town Meeting is on page 8.

Round 5: Payday

Round 6: Shopping

Round 7: "That's Life" Cards
Before you receive your pay, you must take the top card from the pile of "That's Life" cards, which are turned face-down. You must do whatever the card says before you are paid.

Round 8: Payday

Round 9: Shopping

Final Round: Town Meeting
Gather with everyone else and bring some closure to the experience.

Cycle through Rounds 3–9 again as your time permits. Save enough time for the final Town Meeting discussion (pages 8–9).

Cost of Living

Copy and cut apart the lists on this page. Create enough copies to be able to give each student a list of the costs.

Entertainment—$5	Entertainment—$5	Entertainment—$5
Food—$10	Food—$10	Food—$10
Rent—$20	Rent—$20	Rent—$20
Car—$30	Car—$30	Car—$30
College Education—$80	College Education—$80	College Education—$80
House—$90	House—$90	House—$90
Retirement—$100	Retirement—$100	Retirement—$100

Proof of Purchase

Copy and cut apart each of these. Make enough so that you can give a "proof of purchase" each time a student buys something.

Entertainment—$5	Entertainment—$5	Entertainment—$5
Food—$10	Food—$10	Food—$10
Food—$10	Food—$10	Food—$10
Rent—$20	Rent—$20	Rent—$20
Rent—$20	Rent—$20	Rent—$20
Car—$30	Car—$30	Car—$30
College Education—$80	College Education—$80	College Education—$80
House—$90	House—$90	House—$90
Retirement—$100	Retirement—$100	Retirement—$100

Instructions

Photocopy as many of these "That's Life" cards as you think you'll need. Cut them out, shuffle them, and then pile them face-down at the Bank. One card is blank so that you may customize it. You might even make several additional cards from the blank.

Each student picks from the top of the deck during Round 5. He or she reads the card aloud and then must do whatever it says.

Notice that one of the cards says something that affects everyone (Groups A, B, and C), not just one individual. In other words, when someone picks that card, he or she reads it aloud to the whole class. Then everyone must do what it says.

That's Life

Your car breaks down on the way to work. You must pay the Bank $10 to get it fixed if you're going to earn the extra $5 in pay this round. If you can't pay up, $5 will be removed from your basic income this round unless you own or purchase another car.

If you don't have a car: The cost of public transportation has risen, pay an additional $5 toward your bus pass.

That's Life

Your youngest child has to go in for emergency surgery. You must pay the out-of-pocket expenses yourself by giving the Bank $20 this round. If you can't, you will not receive a paycheck at the next round.

That's Life

Your boss has been happy with your work performance and has offered you a raise. Collect $5 more at each Payday from now on.

That's Life

Your college/vocational school payment (or education loan repayment) has come due. Pay the Bank $40 for the next two Paydays.

That's Life

Everyone: A hurricane has destroyed many houses and businesses in your area, including the building in which you live. If you rent an apartment, turn in your rent card and pay the Bank $10 for a down payment on your next apartment, for which you must pay full rent the next shopping round. If you own a house, pay the Bank $50 to cover the damages at this round and hope to get the money back from your insurance company at the next pay period.

That's Life

SESSION 3 — THINKING THEOLOGICALLY

Reason

Goals for This Session

To give students a reality check about credit card debt, investing, budgeting, tithing, and gambling.

To discuss from a Christian perspective what they discovered.

"Skeptics may argue that answered prayers are only coincidences, but as an English archbishop once observed, 'It's amazing how many coincidences occur when one begins to pray.'"

—Bill Hybels, in Too Busy Not to Pray

Prayer Notes

Prayers for the students and their families . . .

Prayers for myself . . .

Prayers for the message itself to have an impact . . .

Other concerns . . .

Activity	Time	Preparation	Supplies
GATHERING			
Gain, Save, Give All You Can	10–15 minutes	None	student books, paper, pencils
Sticky-Note Ritual	3–4 minutes	None	student books
Thinking Theologically	5–7 minutes	None	none
DIVING IN			
OPTION 1 — Focus on Tithing, Credit Card Debt, Investing	20–30 minutes	If you choose to use the Microsoft Excel® spreadsheet for the investing focus, work out the answers for yourself and try a few variations. The spreadsheet is found at www.ileadyouth.com/ILeadYouth _Images_PDF/thinkingmoney.xls.	student books, calculators, paper, pencils, computer with Internet access and Microsoft Excel® (optional)
OPTION 2 — Playing the Lottery	20–30 minutes	Prepare for the American Game (pages 7–9, 11–14).	none
CLOSING			
Think About It	5–10 minutes	None	student books
Worship	3–5 minutes	None	student books

"Having, first, gained all you can, and secondly saved all you can, then 'give all you can.'"
—John Wesley

Gain, Save, Give All You Can

As students arrive, show them the statement by John Wesley on page 28 pf the student book. Hand out paper and pencils and invite the the students to use their reasoning power to grapple with the following questions. You may want to have them form and work in small groups as they come and then report.

1. Why is it smart, or wise, to "gain all you can"? What are the dangers of that philosophy? What are the possibilities for good?

2. Why is it smart, or wise, to "save all you can"? Again, what are the dangers of this philosophy? And what are the possibilities for good?

3. Finally, what does it mean to "give all you can"? Is that generally considered smart or wise? Why, or why not? What are the benefits to such giving—not only for others, but also for you?

Sticky-Note Ritual

Remind the class of the weekly ritual from page 6 in the student book.

Leader: O give thanks to the Lord, for [God] is good,

Class: for [God's] steadfast love endures forever (Psalm 136:1).

Join in prayer, which can be student-led or ad-libbed, or use the following:

Dear Lord, we know the commandment to love you with all of our heart, with all our soul, and with all our mind. Too often we forget that our common sense and intellect are gifts from you, and we instead fill our minds with half-truths and trash. Help us to use our reason in ways that glorify you, especially in the wise use of the money you have entrusted to us. For the sake of your Son, our Savior, Jesus Christ, Amen.

Reason—
Common sense, logic, intellect, using your mind

Thinking Theologically

Again, new students may have joined your class, or students may have forgotten what they learned from week to week. If possible, invite volunteers to go through the four sections of the Wesleyan Quadrilateral as a review for the whole class. Then ask, by way of reminder, "Why is it important to use all four parts of the Quadrilateral—not just 'experience' or 'reason' alone—when discerning God's best for us?"

After some discussion, ask: "What did we focus on last week? [experience] What were the highlights?" And then finally say: "This week we are focusing on the use of 'reason' in relation to how we use our money. What is 'reason'? We learn a lot by our personal experiences with money, but we also can reach conclusions by looking at the facts or statistics and making wise choices based on those. So let's dive in!"

Option 1 in this section is rich with possibilities. Use one session to work with small groups that each take a particular focus, or use more than one session to have the students work with more than one topic.

Option 2 looks at the issue of gambling, which is both a personal issue and a social justice issue.

Feel free to spend more than one session on these topics if you like.

OPTION 1 — Focus on Tithing, Credit Card Debt, Investing, Budgeting

Divide the class into at least four groups of no more than three students. **If your class is small**, pick one or two of the focus areas to do together as a whole group. **If your class is very large**, form multiple groups, as needed, around the four focus areas.

Give each group one of the four areas of focus found on pages 19–26 in the student book to work on together. Make sure each group has a writing utensil and a calculator. Have each group select one person who will write down the group's responses, one or two who will do the math, and one who will report on their work to the rest of the class. (The same person can do more than one task.) Give each group about ten minutes to work on its focus and then bring everyone back together again to report.

Each group should give a summary of its focus area, the answers the group came up with, and a fairly good defense of those answers. Feel free to ask clarifying questions as the reports are given. When all of the groups have reported (about 15 minutes), spend another 15 minutes or so discussing some of the questions at the end of each scenario in the student book. Does the class agree with the conclusions of that group? Why, or why not?

If you have a class of younger students, you may want to explore the issue of "owing your parents money" rather than the issue of credit card debt (see student book pages 20–22). Ask questions such as,

• How many of you have friends who owe their parents money (without naming names)?

• How much money do they owe their parents? What are they doing to pay it off?

• Do you think that it is a good thing to borrow money from your parents? Why, or why not? What does this have to do wit the Bible's commandment to us to honor our parents?

See pages 19–22 for answers to the four scenarios.

Note

The reason that 8% is used in the investing example is that most financial advisors recommend planning for retirement using an 8% figure when investing in the stock market. Between 1942 and 1994, the average compound annual gain was 8.16% per year (www.investorguide.com/cgi-bin/browse2.cgi?back=http://www.investorguide.com/markethistory.html&site=http://cpcug.org/user/invest/bigpic2.html).

For an easier, precise, and flexible approach to this problem, use the Microsoft Excel® spreadsheet found at www.ileadyouth.com/ILeadYouth_Images_PDF/thinkingmoney.xls.

Playing the Lottery

Gambling is a menace to society, deadly to the best interests of moral, social, economic, and spiritual life, and destructive to good government. As an act of faith and concern, Christians should abstain from gambling and strive to minister to those victimized by the practice.

—From The Book of Discipline of The United Methodist Church— 2000, ¶163G.

Play "The American Game" (pages 7–9, 11–14) as before (or if your class hasn't played it yet, introduce the game to them), except with a twist. From the beginning, inform the students that they may play the lottery every time they shop and can buy as many tickets as they wish. Tickets cost $1. For each ticket they buy, they roll 5 dice only once to see if the total adds up to 30, in which case, they win $200. Do not inform them that if they win, they don't receive the money until the next round of "Payday," and that there will be $25 subtracted for tax purposes (you can point that out to the group after the game is over). Inform the bankers to keep track of all the money that comes in for lottery tickets.

At the final "Town Meeting" have the class turn to page 27 in the student book to discuss the issue of gambling.

For further discussion, ask:

- How much money was ultimately spent on the lottery during this game?

- What could have been done with that money?

- Who spent the most money on the lottery? Why?

- If they hadn't spent their money on the lottery, what could they have done with it?

- You may know someone who has lost money gambling or is deep in credit card debt—or debt of any kind. What should your response be to someone in financial trouble? Should you help them? If so, how?

Think About It!

Have students look over the "Think About It!" points on page 28. Invite the students to share some of the highlights of today's session.

Worship

Let your students know that you are excited about what will be happening next week (don't hesitate to explain the plan for the series), and that you are looking forward to what God will be doing in each of their lives as you go through this study together. Ask if there are any prayer requests before inviting a student to lead in prayer.

Close with the liturgy from page 6 in the student book:

Together: May "the grace of the Lord Jesus Christ, the love of God, and the fellowship of the Holy Spirit be with you all." Amen.

—2 Corinthians 13:14

If there is time, have the students work on memorizing the benediction together before they leave. Invite a student to lead the closing worship next week. Remind the youth to take their handouts as they leave.

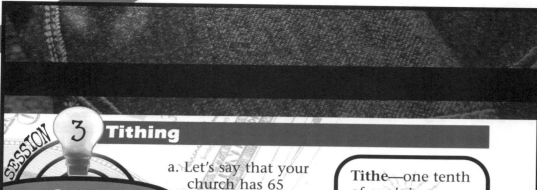

Reason

a. Let's say that your church has 65 families, each earning an average of $45,000 per year. Let's also say that based on the giving, the church budget is $100,000. What percentage of it's income is each family giving to the church?

b. If each family were giving ten percent, how much would the church budget be?

c. If $100,000 covers the church's necessary expenses, including building and grounds, staff salaries, and program supplies, what could the rest of the budget go toward—assuming that everyone tithes ten percent?

d. Researcher George Barna's website (*www.barna.org*) states that "More Americans claim to tithe than actually do: 17% of adults claim to tithe while 6% actually do so (2000)." What is your reaction to those statistics? What do you think contributes to that discrepancy?

e. Why do you think people don't give ten percent in the first place? Do you think that they should? Why, or why not?

f. George Barna's website also states that the younger persons are "the less likely they are to donate any money at all, to donate to a church, and the less money they donate when they do give." What is your reaction to that statement? What do you think contributes to that statistic? How about you? What would it take for you to tithe?

> **Tithe**—one tenth of one's income; see also Leviticus 27:30-32.

Bonus Project
Find out your church's actual statistics: number of families, average income, and church budget. What would your church budget be if everyone tithed ten percent of his or her income? Put together a report for your pastor and leadership board.

Answers
a. Each family is giving about 3.4% of their income.

(Dividing $100,000 by 65 families = $1,538.46. That's how much each family is giving to the church. Then determine what percent of 45,000 is 1,538.46. Use the classic formula: X over [divided by] 100 = 1,538.46 over [divided by] 45,000. Cross multiplying leaves you with 153,846 over [divided by] 45,000, which equals 3.4.)

b. If each family were giving 10 %, the church budget would be $292,500.

(Multiply $45,000 by .10 = $4,500. That is how much each individual family would tithe. Multiply $4,500 by 65 families to arrive at $292,500.)

For the rest of the questions, let the students brainstorm ideas.

Answers

1. Let's say that the students choose to pay off $200/month.

2. $1,374 is the total of the next bill.

a. $1,400 (total) - $200 (payment) = $1,200 (balance)

b. $1,200 (balance) × .145 (interest % rate) = $174 (interest)

c. $1,200 (balance) + $174 (interest) = $1,374 (the total of the next bill)

3. $1,344.23 will be the next bill.

d. $1,374 (this month's bill) - $200 (monthly payment) = $1,174 (balance)

e. $1,174 (balance) × .145 (interest % rate) = $170.23 (interest).

f. $1,174 (balance) + $170.23 (interest) = $1,344.23

4. It will take you 17 months to pay off the computer, from the first payment to the last. (Have the students complete the above formula [d–f], keeping track of the interest and balance amounts in separate columns on paper.)

5. You will have paid $1,814.37 in interest, and a total of $3,214.37 for the computer. (Add the amounts in the interest column [see 4 above], and then add the interest total to the original price of $1400.)

> Owe no one anything, except to love one another; for the one who loves another has fulfilled the law.
>
> —Romans 13:8

 Given your current income and expenses (see page 18), how much will you choose to pay toward your credit card bill each month? (You must make at least the minimum payment of $15.)

 How much will the bill amount be next month?

A. Subtract the amount of your monthly payment from $1400.

= _____

B. Multiply the amount in Line A times the interest rate (.145).

= _____

C. Add lines A and B.

= _____

That's the total of your next bill.

 What will the bill amount be the following month?

D. Subtract your monthly payment from Line C above.

= _____

E. Multiply the amount in Line D times the interest rate (.145).

= _____

F. Add lines D and E.

= _____

That's the total of your next bill.

 Using the formula above to determine your bill each month, how long will it take you to pay off the computer?

 How much will you have paid in interest? How much will you have paid for the computer all together?

2.1

Investing

Christians haven't always been in agreement on the issue of investing. On the one hand, your money could be used to help people who need it now. On the other hand, the money you make off of your investment could be used to help a great many more people down the road. Take some time to discuss:

• Should Christians invest their money or give it away now to someone who needs it?

Jesus told an interesting parable about the good stewards who invested their master's money, or "talents" (Matthew 25:14-28). Most people think that investing is a good thing to do, but they often wait years before they get started. And some, like the third servant in the parable, don't invest at all.

• What is the wisdom behind investing?

• If we do invest, for what do you think God wants us to use our investments?

The basic concept behind investing is simple:

You loan a company money, the company uses that money to improve the business and make larger profits, and you get a share of the profits if the company does well. If the company does poorly, you lose money on your investment. However, a basic rule of thumb for investing is that your money will double every seven years. Thus, if people wish to make a fair amount of money over the long term, they invest in a mutual fund (or group of companies) and keep their money in that fund for dozens of years, regularly adding to it.

So let's get practical. . . .

23

Answers

a. If the rate of growth begins at 8% and stays constant throughout your life, $800 invested on your 16th birthday and compounded annually will grow to $51,047 by your 70th birthday. At an 8% interest rate, your money doubles about every 9 years. See below. (70 -16 = 54)

$800—Start
$1,660 after 9 years
$3,200 after 18 years
$6,400 after 27 years
$12,800 after 36 years
$25,600 after 45 years
$51,200 after 54 years

b. Investing $800 at 8% interest at age 30, you will have only $17,380 when you retire at 70.

c. Invite the students to tell their responses.

d. **Bonus Project**
Investing $800 at 8% interest at age 16 and adding $100 a year every year on your birthday, you will have $129,559 when you retire at 70.

If you are using the Excel® spreadsheet, as another bonus have the students play with several average interest rates and initial investments, such as a 15 year old investing $1,000 at 12%. How much at age 70? ($500,000+)

For an easier, precise, and flexible approach to this problem, use the Microsoft Excel® spreadsheet found at *www.ileadyouth.com/ILeadYouth_Images_PDF/thinkingmoney.xls*.

Answers

a. You will earn $960 per month. (Multiply $8 per hour times 30 hours per week, times 4 weeks in a month.)

b. Your income per month after taxes is $758.40. (Multiplying $960 times .21 [percent of your income that will go for taxes] = $201.60. Subtract $201.60 from $960 to arrive at $758.40, which is what you have left over after taxes.)

c. You pay $206 per month on your car. (Add all the items in letter c.) A suggested plan is to set aside $50 per month on repairs.

d. No, you cannot afford to rent.

Have the students brainstorm ideas for d, e, and f.

.

Budgeting

You and two of your friends have decided to strike out on your own and get your own place. You start searching the classifieds for 2-bedroom apartments. The most reasonable price you can find is $650, utilities included. It requires a deposit equal to one month's rent (which you will get back when you move out, barring any serious damage to the apartment). Before you make a deposit, though, you realize that you should probably create a budget to decide how much you can afford to spend on rent.

So here are your vital statistics:

A. You have a job at which you work 30 hours a week, earning $8 an hour. What is your income per month?

= _____

Your friends are earning about the same amount.

B. You can plan to pay about 21 percent in taxes. (You'll get much of it back early the following year, but that doesn't help much at the moment.) What is your income per month after taxes?

= _____

C. Last year you bought a car, which you will not have paid off until next year. Your monthly car payments are $91 per month, with car insurance at $80 per month and $35 per month on gas. How much are you spending per month on your car?

= _____

What should you plan to set aside for car repairs?

= _____

Total for C = _____

25

Thinking Theologically About ...

SESSION 4

THINKING THEOLOGICALLY

Scripture

Goals for this Session

To teach a formula to help students view any topic through the eyes of Scripture:

- What was God's original intent?
- How did the Fall distort it?
- How did the Cross transform it?
- How are we now to live?

"Father, hallowed be your name. Your kingdom come. Give us each day our daily bread. And forgive us our sins."
—Luke 11:1-4a (NRSV)

Prayer Notes

Prayers for the students and their families . . .

Prayers for myself . . .

Prayers for the message itself to have an impact . . .

Other concerns . . .

Activity	Time	Preparation	Supplies
GATHERING			
What Do You Know?	10–15 minutes	None	student books, large sheets of paper, markers, Bibles and/or Bible concordances (optional)
Sticky-Note Ritual	3–4 minutes	None	student books
Thinking Theologically	5–10 minutes	None	student books
DIVING IN			
OPTION 1 **In-depth Study**	20–30 minutes	None	Bibles, student books, paper, pencils
OPTION 2 **Creative Response**	20–30 minutes	None	Bibles, student books, paper, pencils, posterboard or large paper, markers and/or crayons
CLOSING			
Think About It	7–10 minutes	None	student books
Worship	3–5 minutes	None	student books

Money

What Do You Know?

As the students arrive, engage them in creating a list of all of the biblical stories or phrases the students can think of that mention money, possessions, or greed. The stories don't actually have to be primarily about one of those three things; the passage must simply have some mention of it. List everything the students say, whether or not it's actually biblical (come back to it later). They may list Old Testament stories, parables, stories about Jesus, passages from Paul's letters, proverbs, and so on.

Have the students summarize the passages for the whole class, in case some have never heard the reference before. If you wish, give each student a Bible and/or a concordance and have him or her skim various sections of it to find a passage making reference to money, possessions, or greed. Subtopics could include riches, wealth, laziness, dishonest gain, waste. Proverbs is a great place to start.

After you have a significant list, invite the students to turn to page 29 in the student book. Read together or summarize the information there. You may want to have one of the students write these questions out for the whole class to see:

• What was God's original intent?
• How did the Fall distort it?
• How did the Cross transform it?
• How are we now to live?

Sticky-Note Ritual

Remind the class of the weekly ritual from page 6 in the student book.

Leader: "O give thanks to the LORD, for [God] is good,"

Class: "for [God's] steadfast love endures forever." (Psalm 136:1)

Join briefly in prayer. This can be student-led, or ad-libbed, or you can use the following:

Dear Lord, besides you, there is perhaps no topic more widely discussed in Scripture than stewardship. Give us "ears to hear" what you have to say to us about the wise use of our money. Help us to look at each aspect of the biblical story in such a way that gives us a faithful understanding of your truth. And finally, Lord, empower us by your Holy Spirit to do all that you ask us to, as loving, faithful servants of Jesus Christ. Amen.

Thinking Theologically

Again, new students may have joined your class or students may have forgotten what they learned from week to week. If possible, invite a student to go briefly through the four sections of the Wesleyan Quadrilateral (on page 9 of the student book) as a review for the whole class. Then ask: "What have we focused on in the past few weeks [experience and reason]? What were the highlights?"

After some discussion say: "This week we are going to focus on Scripture with regard to how we use our money. What does the Bible, or Scripture, have to say about the wise use of our resources? Did you know that of the many topics covered in the Bible, stewardship, materialism, and wise use of resources are among the most often mentioned? That's how important the subject of money is. Let's dive in!"

Diving In

The two options below both depend on the students' having a basic grasp of the biblical formula. If you have not already done so, spend a few minutes introducing it, using the information on page 29 in the student book. Ask questions to be sure students understand the meaning of the questions in the formula. For example, you may want to have a volunteer explain "the Fall."

Then choose one of the two options below, or invite students to choose whether they would like to tackle the in-depth study while others do the creative response. Both are valid styles of learning. Be sure to leave time for reporting to the rest of the group.

In-depth Study

Spend the rest of class time going through each part of the formula on pages 29–33 in the student book one at a time. Have the students read the verses and answer the questions on their own, then go through the answers with them before moving on to the next part. For the third part, you may wish to divide the students into pairs to look up one or two gospel passages from the list, then have them report to the rest of the group. If the group gets bogged down in the details, continually bring them back to the "big picture," asking those four key questions.

Creative Response

Divide the students into four groups, giving each group one of the four parts of the biblical formula on pages 29–33 in the student book. Once they have spent time reading the passages and answering the questions, have them either create a skit or make a poster that depicts their part of the biblical formula and how it relates to money. Then have the groups present their skits or posters to the rest of the class. The only rule for this activity is that they must involve every person in their group in either the production of the skit or the creation of the poster.

Think About It

Discuss the highlights of this session. What did the students learn that they didn't know before? What really jumped out at them from the Scripture passages? How will they apply these truths from Scripture to their everyday lives?

Turn to page 34 in the student book, and go through the questions together.

Worship

Let the students know that you are excited about what will be happening next week and that you are looking forward to what God will be doing in each of their lives as you go through this study together. Ask if there are any prayer requests before inviting a student to lead in prayer.

Close with the liturgy from page 6 in the student book:

Together: May "the grace of the Lord Jesus Christ, the love of God, and the fellowship of the Holy Spirit be with all of you." Amen.
—2 Corinthians 13:14

Thinking Theologically About . . .

Why did Adam and Eve have no need for money in the garden?
Adam and Eve had no need for money in the garden because God provided for all their needs directly.

What does that tell you about God's original intent?
God's original intent was that humans would rely on God to supply all of their needs.

What did their stewardship of God's creation entail?
See Genesis 1:28; 2:15.

What Was God's Original Intent?

Read Genesis 1:26-30.

God created men and women in God's "image" and made them "good." There was nothing separating God from humans; they could talk and interact with God in perfect communion. God set them as "stewards" over the whole earth and provided everything they needed.

- Why did Adam and Eve have no need for money in the garden?

- What does that tell you about God's original intent for humankind and their use of money/resources?

- What did their stewardship of God's creation entail (Genesis 2:15)?

How Did "the Fall" Distort It?

Read Genesis 3.

The "Fall" is a theological and practical term for when humankind (Adam and Eve) first chose to disobey God's instructions. In fact, they disobeyed God because they wanted to have, have, have! From that moment on, sin separated humankind from God, affecting their lives and the lives of all their descendants, including us (Romans 5:12-14). In the Old Testament view, sin required sacrifice to obtain forgiveness. The Fall not only affects our communion with God and with one another, but also distorts our role as stewards of all creation, leading to sinful use of our money, our resources, and our environment.

- After the Fall, how were humans' needs met (food, shelter, clothing)?

30

Why do you think God commanded the people to tithe from the land?
God commanded God's people to tithe from the land as a constant, visible reminder of their reliance on God for all of their provisions.

What examples have you seen that point to the sinfulness of humankind in their use of money, resources, and the environment?
Have the students tell their own responses based on their own experiences. Examples might be gambling, toxic waste, greed.

Read Genesis 4:1-12.

• How soon after the Fall do we find people giving offerings to God? Why do you think they began this practice?

• What sort of offering or sacrifice did God find acceptable? Why?

Abraham was the first to give a tenth, or a "tithe," to a priest of God (Genesis 14:17-20). Later Moses recorded God's commandment to tithe in Leviticus 27:30. This set the Old Testament standard for many centuries.

• Why do you think God commanded the people to tithe from the land? What value did it have for the people to do this?

God also commanded God's people to offer ceremonial sacrifices of animals and produce. This was the primary function of the priests in the tabernacle, and eventually the primary activity in the Temple in Jerusalem.

These offerings were in five categories: burnt offerings, grain offerings, fellowship (or free-will) offerings, sin offerings, and guilt offerings. By the time Jesus arrived on the scene, the priests and teachers of the Law had added many little rules to the ritualistic offerings; and the exchange of money for the selling of sacrificial animals had become a booming business in the outer area of the Temple. We never see Jesus angrier than when he confronts this behavior (John 2:13-16).

• What examples have you seen that point to the sinfulness of humankind in their use of their money, resources, and the environment?

31

How Did the Cross Transform It?

The "Cross" refers to the manner in which Jesus died—on a Roman cross, as a sacrifice for the sins of the whole world. His death broke the power of sin, and his Resurrection broke the power of death. Sin and death are the two main enemies of humankind. Because of his sacrificial death, the ritualistic offerings were no longer necessary (Hebrews 10:11-14).

Before his death and resurrection, Jesus spent a lot of time talking about the kingdom of God, as well as the wise use of our money and resources. Look up two passages from this list:

• Based on these passages, what would you say is Jesus' opinion about money and the use of our resources?

Matthew 6:19-21
Matthew 17:24-27
Matthew 20:1-16
Matthew 23:23-24
Mark 10: 17-31
Mark 12:41-44
Luke 7:36-47
Luke 12: 13-21
Luke 16:10-15
Luke 19:1-10

• Look at Jesus' lifestyle. He kept things simple. He came from a poor family. He had no home and few belongings. He and his disciples ate what was offered to them by hospitable hosts, or they gleaned what they could in the fields. Jesus often hung out with the poor and the outcasts of his day. What example does that set for his followers, for us?

32

Based on these passages, what would you say is Jesus' opinion about money and the use of our resources?
Jesus did not have a home or many possessions, but he often relied on the resources of others for his food and housing. He encouraged his followers to trust in God for everything, and not wear themselves out trying to accumulate things that did not last.

What example does [Jesus] set for his followers, for us?
Based on Jesus' example, Christians are to live simply, befriend the poor, and trust God for their daily provisions—rather than pursue materialism.

What did the early Christians give up? ...
The early Christians gave up money and property, probably surprising—maybe even frustrating—their friends and family. However, they were able to help the poor when all those resources were pooled together.

What is "real life"?
"Real life" is recognizing that we are not in control—God is in control, and we are to trust God for everything.

What would James say?
James might say, "Life is short. Don't wait before doing as much good as you can. People need to see that God is real."

How are we to live?
Let the students come up with their own answers based on all they have studied.

For Further Discussion
Review the students' list of Bible passages. Address any that are not actually from the Bible. Two well-known sayings often attributed to the Bible are "Money is the root of all evil" and "God helps those who help themselves." The verse from 1 Timothy 6:10 actually says, *"The love of* money is the root of all evil [emphasis ours]"; and the other saying is nowhere to be found in Scripture. You may want to have a concordance handy for students to try to find the verses they mentioned.

> "You received without payment, give without payment."
> —Matthew 10:8

How Are We Now to Live?

Jesus' life, death, and resurrection paved the way for the transforming power of the Holy Spirit in the life of every believer. We are no longer to be slaves to what the world values but to be servants in the kingdom of God—giving joyfully and freely in loving obedience to what God asks. For the early Christians this meant a truly radical lifestyle—not just tithing.

• **Read Acts 2:43-47 and Acts 4:32-35.** What did the early Christians give up? Why? How do you think their neighbors, friends, and family members reacted to that lifestyle? What were the early Christians able to accomplish for the kingdom of God?

• The apostle Paul wrote instructions to Timothy, the young pastor of the church in Ephesus (1 Timothy 6:6-10, 17-19). What do you think Paul means by the phrase "that they may take hold of the life that really is life"? Compare that to what Jesus says in John 10:10. What is "real life"?

• The writer of the book of James also takes a counter-cultural view (James 4:13-17). What would James have to say to someone who says and believes that "Life is short. Spend all your money however you want"?

• How are we now to live as modern-day followers of Jesus?

33

SESSION 5

THINKING THEOLOGICALLY

Tradition

Goals for this Session

To understand the church's historical stance on money.

To examine different approaches that Christians of many denominations have taken on money.

Unless in the first waking moment of the day you learn to fling the door wide back and let God in, you will work on a wrong level all day; but swing the door wide open and pray to your Father in secret, and every public thing will be stamped with the presence of God.

—Oswald Chambers in My Utmost for His Highest

Activity	Time	Preparation	Supplies
GATHERING			
What Is Tradition?	10–15 minutes	None	none
Sticky-Note Ritual	3–4 minutes	None	student books
Thinking Theologically	7–10 minutes	None	student books
DIVING IN			
OPTION 1 **Tradition and Today**	20–30 minutes	Determine how many game cards your class will need. Then photocopy pages 35 and 37, cut out the cards, and stack them in two piles according to which page they were on.	student books, posterboard or large sheets of paper, markers, paper, pencils, camera with film, tape
OPTION 2 **Where Do We Stand?**	20–30 minutes	Invite your pastor to class and/or have on hand denominational materials. Determine how many game cards your class will need. Then photocopy pages 36 and 37, cut out the cards, and stack them in two piles according to which page they were on.	student books, markerboard, posterboard or large sheets of paper, markers, paper, pencils, camera with film, tape
CLOSING			
Think About It	7–10 minutes	None	student books
Worship	3–5 minutes	None	student books

Prayer Notes

Prayers for the students and their families . . .

Prayers for myself . . .

Prayers for the message itself to have an impact . . .

Other concerns . . .

Money

Tradition—
Practices and learnings of the church that have stood the test of time as valid and that shape the thinking and actions of people in the present

What's Tradition?

As students arrive, invite them to tell stories of family, school, or church traditions that they especially enjoy. Ask questions about how long the tradition has been going on, how it got started, if the meaning today is the same as in earlier times, and so on.

Introduce the definition of tradition as it relates to the church.

Sticky-Note Ritual

Remind the class of the weekly ritual, on page 6 in the student book.

Leader: O give thanks to the Lord, for [God] is good,

Class: for [God's] steadfast love endures forever (Psalm 136:1).

Join briefly in prayer. This can be student-led or ad-libbed, or use the following:

Dear Lord, thank you for the privilege of worshipping in this church and learning from the saints who have gone before us. Give us open hearts to all they teach and to the traditions they have handed down to us. Help us to be faithful to our heritage so that future generations may see living examples of what Christians are called to be in Jesus Christ—particularly in the wise use of our money and resources. For the sake of your Son our Savior, Jesus Christ, Amen.

Thinking Theologically

Review what your class has studied in the previous weeks. If possible, invite one or more students to go through the four sections of the Quadrilateral (on page 9) as a review for the whole class. Then ask: "What have we focused on in the past few weeks? [experience, reason, and Scripture] What were the highlights?"

After some discussion say, "This week we are going to focus on the last section of the Quadrilateral, 'tradition.' What has been the Christian church's relationship with money throughout history? What are the different Christian traditions with regard to the wise use of our money and resources?"

If you choose Option 2 in "Diving In," pose these questions also:

• What does our denomination, in particular, have to say about it?
• How does that make us different from other denominations, with regard to money?
• How well is our local church doing in terms of following our denominational stance on the use of money?

Say, "Let's dive in!"

The two options use different viewpoints on church tradition as their starting points—one historical; the other, the classic Neibuhr *Christ and Culture* paradigm. It is less important that students master the facts than it is that they grapple with how church tradition interacts with how Christians make day-to-day decisions.

Use one or both of the challenges, as your time and interest dictate. You may choose to spend more than one class period if you would like to do both.

Tradition and Today

Invite everyone to turn to page 35 in the student book. To introduce this study, say: "Throughout the centuries, Christians have taken a variety of approaches to the issues of stewardship and materialism. Your student book gives us a historical glance at those approaches, from the early church to today. You'll notice that the various approaches can be contradictory. Should one be separate from the world, or part of it? Let's take a look."

Have students read pages 35–36 and make notes in their books to identify instances that answer the two questions. Then together compare and contrast the church's tradition. Make a list on the board.

Have the students divide into groups of at least three. Have on hand the appropriate number of cards (pages 35 and 37), which you have already photocopied, cut out, and stacked into two piles. Give these instructions:

"For the next activity we are going to explore some of the different Christian views on how we are to interact with the world. A representative from each group will pick one Historical Overview card from the left-hand stack (from page 35). Those cards represent one of the Christian views. Then a representative from each group will pick one card from the right-hand stack (from page 37). Those cards represent an everyday money problem. It is then your group's challenge to come up with a skit or poster that represents how the Christian perspective on the one card would interact with the money problem on the other." (Give the groups a time limit.)

Then send them to work. As with previous sessions, bring the groups back to present their skits and posters for the last few minutes of class. Have fun with this option! Take photographs of the skits, and hang up the posters around the classroom for the next few weeks.

Where Do We Stand?

Before class: Invite your pastor to attend the session or to give you materials that will provide the information you need about your denomination's position on these issues.

Spend a few minutes going over pages 37 and 40 of the student book, reading aloud or summarizing on a large sheet of paper or markerboard.

The glossary of terms, on page 40, may be helpful in these discussions.

Ask questions such as: "What names do you recognize here? Do you recognize any faith traditions or denominations here? Have you ever met anyone who held that particular view? Where is our denomination represented?"

Ask the pastor the questions on page 41 of the student book. If your pastor is not able to attend, use any denominational resources you have gathered, or spend some time researching on the Internet. You may also photocopy and review together the Confessions of the Church (page 38), asking yourself, "What Christian view does this confession of faith represent?"

If you have time, divide the students into groups of at least three. Have on hand the appropriate number of cards (pages 36 and 37), which you have already photocopied, cut out, and stacked into two piles. Give these instructions:

"For the next activity we are going to explore some of the different Christian views on how we are to interact with the world. A representative from each group will pick one card from the left-hand stack (from page 36). Those cards represent one of the Christian views. Then a representative from each group will pick one card from the right-hand stack (from page 37). Those cards represent an everyday money problem. It is then your group's challenge to come up with a skit or poster that represents how the Christian perspective on the one card would interact with the money problem on the other." (Give the students a time limit.)

Then send them to work. As with previous sessions, bring the groups back to present their skits and posters for the last few minutes of class. Have fun with this option! Take photographs of the skits, and hang the posters up around the classroom for the next few weeks.

Think About It

Have the students look over the "Think About It" points on page 42. Ask what the highlights of this session were. Encourage students to identify their points of personal connection.

Worship

Let your students know that you are proud of all they have accomplished in the past few weeks, and that you look forward to one final session with them on the topic of money. Suggest that they pray about the one or two things they might change about the way they use their money after studying this topic and that they come next week prepared to share. Ask if there are any prayer requests before inviting a student to lead in prayer.

Close with the liturgy from page 6 in the student book:

Together: May "the grace of the Lord Jesus Christ, the love of God, and the fellowship of the Holy Spirit be with all of you." Amen.

—2 Corinthians 13:14

Historical Overview

Card A: The Prophetic Reformers

Martin Luther and John Calvin (1500s), Karl Barth (1930s), and the contemporary Tony Campolo challenged the unbiblical financial practices of the established church and the materialistic culture in which the church operated.

Card B: Separation from the World

Quakers, Mennonites, and folks like George Fox (1600s) emphasized complete separation from the world and all that it offers.

Card C: Incarnational Missions

Missionaries Amy Carmichael and J. Hudson Taylor (1800s) emphasized taking on the lifestyle of those they served, in food, dress, household items, and so forth. However, they were quick to identify those things in culture that were ungodly.

Card D: Gospel of Prosperity

Some TV evangelists such as Jim and Tammy Bakker (1970s and '80s) promised that if a person gave to their ministry, God would bless that person with health and wealth.

Card A: The Prophetic Reformers

Martin Luther and John Calvin (1500s), Karl Barth (1930s), and the contemporary Tony Campolo challenged the unbiblical financial practices of the established church and the materialistic culture in which the church operated.

Card B: Separation from the World

Quakers, Mennonites, and folks like George Fox (1600s) emphasized complete separation from the world and all that it offers.

Card C: Incarnational Missions

Missionaries Amy Carmichael and J. Hudson Taylor (1800s) emphasized taking on the lifestyle of those they served, in food, dress, household items, and so forth. However, they were quick to identify those things in culture that were ungodly.

Card D: Gospel of Prosperity

Some TV evangelists such as Jim and Tammy Bakker (1970s and '80s) promised that if a person gave to their ministry, God would bless that person with health and wealth.

Christ and Culture

Card A: Christ of Culture

This view says that the world is good. Christ is in all cultures. You can be part of culture and enjoy all that it has to offer. Traditions within this category include Gnostics, old liberals, and Marxist Christians. Key figures include Thomas Jefferson, Immanuel Kant, and Alfred Lloyd Tennyson.

Card B: Christ Transforms Culture

This view says that the world is both good and evil. Culture is tainted with sin but changeable. The world can be made a better place if sin is dealt with in a meaningful way. Traditions within this category are Calvinists (Reformed, Presbyterian) and Wesleyans (Methodists, holiness traditions). Key figures include St. Augustine, John Calvin, and John Wesley.

Card C: Christ Against Culture

This view says that the world is entirely evil. Christians should not participate in culture; they are to be completely separate. Traditions within this category include Monastic, Mennonite, and Quaker communities, as well as fundamentalist Charismatics. Key figures include Tertullian, St. Benedict, Bob Jones, and Jimmy Swaggart.

Card A: Christ of Culture

This view says that the world is good. Christ is in all cultures. You can be part of culture and enjoy all that it has to offer. Traditions within this category include Gnostics, old liberals, and Marxist Christians. Key figures include Thomas Jefferson, Immanuel Kant, and Alfred Lloyd Tennyson.

Card B: Christ Transforms Culture

This view says that the world is both good and evil. Culture is tainted with sin but changeable. The world can be made a better place if sin is dealt with in a meaningful way. Traditions within this category are Calvinists (Reformed, Presbyterian) and Wesleyans (Methodists, holiness traditions). Key figures include St. Augustine, John Calvin, and John Wesley.

Card C: Christ Against Culture

This view says that the world is entirely evil. Christians should not participate in culture; they are to be completely separate. Traditions within this category include Monastic, Mennonite, and Quaker communities, as well as fundamentalist Charismatics. Key figures include Tertullian, St. Benedict, Bob Jones, and Jimmy Swaggart.

Thinking Theologically About . . .

Everyday Money Problems

Card A

Your pastor announces that the leadership has decided to take out a $1.5 million loan for upgrading the church facility, and everyone needs to make a big pledge. But somewhere you remember reading that the church gave only $5,000 toward missions efforts last year. What is your response? Why?

Card B

A single mother comes to your family needing financial assistance. You know that you have the money to help her, but you also know that she hasn't always been wise in the past about how she spends her money. What is your response? Why?

Card C

You're thinking about joining the team that runs a teen coffeehouse ministry in your church basement. One of the other team members invites you to go shopping with her for "cool clothes" to wear for working at the coffeehouse. What is your response? Why?

Card D

You have some money left over from your paycheck that you would like to give away. There are lots of options: your church building fund, the Humane Society, your friend who owes her parents a lot of money, and the guy in youth group who is going on a mission trip to Cuba. Which do you choose? Why?

Card E

You suddenly realize that you owe your parents more money than you will be able to make in the next three months. That afternoon the church sends you a letter asking for your weekly pledge for the coming year. What do you do? Why?

Card F

You've been invited to rent an apartment with several of your college friends. It would be cheaper than living in the dorms, but you know that two of your friends drink a lot and the other has had his girlfriend over to spend the night several times. What is your response?

Confessions of the Church About Stewardship

These are highlights from various credal statements created over the course of 500 years—from the Reformation to modern times. Creeds prior to the Reformation tended to focus on doctrinal issues rather than Christian lifestyle issues.

Highlights From Martin Luther's 95 Theses (1517)

43. Christians are to be taught that he who gives to the poor or lends to the needy does a better work than buying pardons.
45. Christians are to be taught that he who sees a man in need, and passes him by, and gives [his money] for pardons, purchases not the indulgences of the pope, but the indignation of God.
86. Again: —"Why does not the pope, whose wealth is to-day greater than the riches of the richest, build just this one church of St. Peter with his own money, rather than with the money of poor believers?"

From the Lutheran Confessions (Augsburg Confession, 1530)

What is meant by "daily bread"?

Answer: Everything required to satisfy our bodily needs, such as food and clothing, house and home, fields and flocks, money and property; a pious spouse and good children, trustworthy servants, godly and faithful rulers, good government; seasonable weather, peace and health, order and honor; true friends, faithful neighbors, and the like.

From the English Reformation (The Edwardian Homilies, 1547)

Take no man's goods, nor covet your neighbor's goods wrongfully; but content yourselves with that which ye get truly; and also bestow your own goods charitably, as need and case requireth.

From the Anabaptist Confessions (The Schleitheim Confession, 1527)

The Riches and Goods of Christians are not common, as touching the right, title, and possession of the same; as certain Anabaptists do falsely boast. Notwithstanding, every man ought, of such things as he possesseth, liberally to give alms to the poor, according to his ability.

From the Baptist Creeds of The New Hampshire Confession, 1833

God is the source of all blessings, temporal and spiritual; all that we have and are we owe to him. We have a spiritual debtorship to the whole world, a holy trusteeship in the Gospel, and binding stewardship in our possessions. We are therefore under obligation to serve him with our time, talents and material possessions; and should recognize all these as entrusted to us to use for the glory of God and helping others.

From the Twenty-Five Articles of the Methodist Conference 1784

XXIV. Of Christian Men's Goods.

The riches and goods of Christians are not common, as touching the right, title and possession of the same, as some do falsely boast. Notwithstanding, every man ought, of such things as he possesseth, liberally to give alms to the poor, according to his ability.

From the World Council of Churches, 1948

There are millions who are hungry, millions who have no home, no country and no hope. Over all mankind hangs the peril of total war. We have to accept God's judgment upon us for our share in the world's guilt. Often we have tried to serve God and mammon, put other loyalties before loyalty to Christ, confused the Gospel with our own economic or national or racial interests, and feared war more than we have hated it. As we have talked with one another here, we have begun to understand how our separation has prevented us from receiving correction from one another in Christ. And because we lacked this correction, the world has often heard from us not the Word of God but the words of men.

From The Confession of the United Presbyterian Church in the United States of America, 1967

The reconciliation of man through Jesus Christ makes it plain that enslaving poverty in a world of abundance is an intolerable violation of God's good creation. Because Jesus identified himself with the needy and exploited, the cause of the world's poor is the cause of his disciples. The church cannot condone poverty, whether it is the product of unjust social structures, exploitation of the defenseless, lack of national resources, absence of technological understanding, or rapid expansion of populations. The church calls every man to use his abilities, his possessions, and the fruits of technology as gifts entrusted to him by God for the maintenance of his family and the advancement of the common welfare. It encourages those forces in human society that raise men's hopes for better conditions and provide them with opportunity for a decent living.

From the Social Creed of The United Methodist Church, from The Book of Discipline of the United Methodist Church, 2000

We believe in the right and duty of persons to work for the glory of God and the good of themselves and others and in the protection of their welfare in so doing; in the rights to property as a trust from God, collective bargaining, and responsible consumption; and in the elimination of economic and social distress.

And from the social policies and resolutions of the same:

We claim all economic systems to be under the judgment of God no less than other facets of the created order.

All of the above are from Creeds of the Churches, revised edition, edited by John H. Leith, © 1973 by John Knox Press, with the exception of the excerpts from Martin Luther's 95 Theses and the material from The Book of Discipline of the United Methodist Church, 2000. Copyright © 2000 by the United Methodist Publishing House.

Glossary of Terms

confession—act of confessing; a formulary of articles of faith; a creed

consecrate—to set apart; to make holy

conservative (theologically)—tending toward a more literal interpretation of Scripture; holding traditional Christian beliefs

creed—a system of principles believed or professed; a brief summary of the articles of the Christian faith

fundamentalist (theologically)—characterized by having a strictly literal interpretation of Scripture; having a separatist approach to culture

Gnosticism—a first-century worldview in which the spirit is separate from the body

incarnational—a uniquely theological term referring to the "taking on of flesh" when God became human in Jesus Christ

indulgence—in the medieval Catholic Church, it meant a purchase of pardon for your own or another's sins

liberal (theologically)—tending toward a more symbolic interpretation of Scripture; characterized by nontraditional Christian beliefs and assimilation with culture

martyr—one who is murdered for his or her religious beliefs

Marxism—a worldview based on the teachings of Karl Marx in which there is no God, there are no social classes (no rich or poor); everything is held in common

materialism—a high valuation on the accumulation of money and possessions

Neo-orthodoxy—a theological movement that developed during World Wars I and II as a backlash against liberal theology

sacrificial offering—giving beyond what you can afford

simplicity—a spiritual discipline in which you limit your personal possessions to only those things that you really need

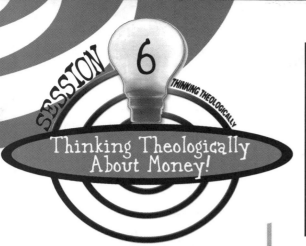

SESSION 6

THINKING THEOLOGICALLY

Thinking Theologically About Money!

Prayer is the discipline of the moment.

—Henri J. M. Nouwen, in Here and Now

Activity	Time	Preparation	Supplies
GATHERING			
Quiz Time	10–15 minutes	None	student books, paper, pencils
Sticky-Note Ritual	1–4 minutes	None	none
Thinking Theologically	7–10 minutes	None	student books
DIVING IN			
OPTION 1 **Going to God**	15–30 minutes	Ask your pastor to do Communion and make sure to have Communion elements on hand. If you are going to have a different Order of Worship than what is printed in the student book, have worship bulletins for all participants.	student books, Bible, basket, music recordings and a player or instruments and musicians (optional), hymnals or songbooks, index cards, pens or pencils, Communion elements, paper if doing journaling (optional)
OPTION 2 **Going to Others**	20–25 minutes	None	paper and pencils or posterboard and markers
CLOSING			
Think About It	10–15 minutes	None	student books
Worship	3–5 minutes	None	student books

Prayer Notes

Prayers for the students and their families . . .

Prayers for myself . . .

Prayers for the message itself to have an impact . . .

Other concerns . . .

Quiz Time

As students arrive, direct them to the questions on page 43. The youth may work individually, in pairs, or in small groups of no more than four students. Incorporate later arrivals into the activity in process.

Sticky-Note Ritual

Convene the class with their "Sticky-Note Ritual." The students should have it memorized by now.

Leader: O give thanks to the Lord, for [God] is good,

Class: for [God's] steadfast love endures forever (Psalm 136:1).

Join in prayer, which can be student-led or ad-libbed; or use the following:

Dear Lord, we are grateful for all you have taught us over the past few weeks. We have been challenged to use our money for your purposes alone, and have been convicted about the ways we have failed to do so. Show us what you have called us to do with our money, and give us the strength through your Spirit to follow through with those commitments. For the sake of your Son, our Savior, Jesus Christ, Amen.

Thinking Theologically

Once the youth have completed the questions and the opening ritual, spend time going over the answers to the quiz. Invite the students to explain what they came up with.

Diving In

The two options below represent two very different styles. Take into account what you know about the group's learning preferences as well as your time and interest.

Both of these options will require preparation well before the session.

Going to God Together and Individually

If you use the Order of Worship provided on pages 44–45 in the student book, make sure every participant has a copy. Begin as soon as most of the class has arrived. Feel free to make additions or changes to the suggested order. (For some ideas, look at the suggestions for journaling on pages 46–47 of the student book.) If you do make changes, provide students with a worship bulletin to help them participate.

Be sure to check with your pastor about who is to serve Communion.

If you choose to use the worship experience (Option 1), you may skip this opening liturgy, as it is incorporated into that experience.

Thinking Theologically About ...

OPTION: As an addition to the worship service or in place of some of its elements, set aside some time for individual journaling. Have the students turn to pages 46–47 in their book. Give paper and pens or pencils to the students. Invite them to find a private place somewhere on the church grounds away from other people (the bathrooms are not an option). They should be at least twenty feet from the nearest person and must commit to silence for the time allotted. Then send them out to their places. When the time is up, circulate again with the news that you will finish as a group back in the classroom. Invite the students to talk about what they came up with for their personal creeds.

OPTION 2 Going to Others

As with previous sessions, divide the students into four groups, giving each group one section from the Wesleyan Quadrilateral, from page 9 in the student book. Have each group take time to either create a skit or make a poster that depicts their part of the Wesleyan Quadrilateral and how it relates to money. Then have the groups present their skits or posters to the rest of the class in order (experience first, then reason, Scripture, and tradition). The only rule for this activity is that they must involve every person in their group in either the production of the skit or the creation of the poster. Have fun with this creative option! Take pictures of the skits and hang the posters up around the room.

Think About It

Invite the students to respond to the questions on page 48. Then read aloud the passage from Thomas G. Pettepiece's book *Visions of a World Hungry* as found on page 47 in the student book. Have students create their own creed or set of questions to use every time they make a decision or a purchase.

Worship

Ask whether there are any prayer requests before leading the group in prayer. Use this time to lift up each student in the class so that they will be empowered by the Holy Spirit to follow through with the commitments they have made.

Close with the liturgy from page 6 in the student book:

Together: May "the grace of the Lord Jesus Christ, the love of God, and the fellowship of the Holy Spirit be with all of you." Amen.

—2 Corinthians 13:14

Encourage the
students to take
their student books
home.

Tough Questions

John Wesley presented the members of his congregation with these questions to challenge their use of money:

(1) In expending this, am I acting according to my character? Am I acting herein, not as a proprietor, but as a steward of my Lord's goods?

(2) Am I doing this in obedience to [God'] Word? In what Scripture does [God] require me to do so?

(3) Can I offer up this action, this expense, as a sacrifice to God through Jesus Christ?

(4) Have I reason to believe that for this very work I shall have a reward at the resurrection of the just?

You will seldom need anything more to remove any doubt which arises on this head; but by this four-fold consideration you will receive clear light as to the way wherein you should go.

—From "The Use of Money," Sermon 50, by John Wesley

Thinking Theologically About ...